Dreaming Again

Poems

Martin Elwell

ISBN: 1494236346
ISBN-13: 978-1494236342

CONTENTS

POEMS OF THE LOST

ACKNOWLEDGMENTS

Sincere thanks to the editors and staff of the publications in which the following poems first appeared:

Specs Journal: "Excel Poem"

Third Wednesday: "Self Portrait, To Ginsberg"

Evening Street Review: "My Sister's Face," "Buttered Popcorn," "Amnesia," "House Arrest," "My Aluminum Baseball Bat," "Snipes"

Convergence Journal: "Lifecycle of a Wasp's Nest," "Day Planner," "Feeding Cycle of the Clock"

Untoward: "Friday Night Binge," "Transcription of a Doctor's Appointment"

Empty Mirror Magazine of the Arts: "Self Portrait, For Kerouac", "Self Portrait, To Ginsberg," "Lady Liberty," "Dedication," "Scribbling," "During Sleep"

I'd also like to thank Janet Sylvester for her input and encouragement throughout the writing of this book.

LONG-SLEEVE WHITE COLLARED SHIRT

Day Planner

I've abandoned moon gazing, beach sitting, napping, meditating
and bird watching.

I've given up on sitting still long enough to watch a candle burn, a campfire
consume itself, snow fall, wind blow, clouds pass, veins pulse
or one foot tap.

I work:

waking, dressing, running, showering, re-dressing, driving,
passing everyone to gain a few seconds, tailgating, speeding,
lane switching…

hand gesturing, radio singing, cell phone talking, text messaging, parking…

saying good morning, key striking, word scanning, ink scribbling
and symmetrically organizing.

I participate:

scrawl notes in meetings to keep my hands moving, take the stairs,
answer questions, respond to e-mails (hundreds of them).

I assign work, manage performance, monitor behavior,
host conference calls, argue, piss, laugh, leave.

I run errands:

food shopping, picking up dry cleaning, complaining, scheming,
worrying about this in order to avoid worrying about that.

I clean dishes, swallow Advil, yawn, fake a smile, my metabolism slows,
my motivation declines.

I download porn, sit on the couch, watch a sitcom, channel surf…
my head nods, my eye lids close,

the moon unlooked at, the beach in darkness, one lark singing somewhere else.

Self Portrait
For Kerouac

In 1947, Jack stepped across the Colorado border
to the flash of a camera.
He stood erect, the shadows of dirt and knuckles
darkening his eyes.

As if the hand of Moses were in Lowell, sun
parted down-pouring clouds in 2004. On my way home
from a job interview in Boston, I stopped
at his grave. I was in a long-sleeve white collared shirt, and Jack

was in the ground, probably
wearing the same thing. I didn't take off my tie.
It dragged in the mud as I dried his stone
to make a charcoal rubbing that now fades in a drawer.

I stood in the rain, the grass and water
darkening the knees of my suit pants, and wrote a poem
on a small square of paper. I dropped it in the grass
next to the empty whiskey bottles left in his honor.

Now, whenever I pull my dry-cleaned clothes from the closet,
I think of Jack waiting for a ride into Utah. I recall kneeling
at his grave, and I remember leaving my ink
to bleed into the ground.

Dreaming Again

Morning traffic, the gentle sway of the back-seat, he's asleep again.
Dreaming of running through city streets, his legs are weak again.

The car enters the anthill commute.
He hopes to wake up an optimist, he wants to believe again.

He disappears into the workday's sexual fantasies and e-mails.
At lunch, crowds and cigarettes, he plots the weekend again.

On Friday night, he'll drink too much; buy the world in pint glasses.
On Saturday, he'll exercise it away; weight-loss scheming again.

This ritual repeats until his pay-check dependency fully develops.
The spin of weeks takes hold, and he's searching for relief again.

He needs a pause, a break, escape from everyday necessities.
Empty stomachs need filling, empty minds distracting. Martin is dreaming again.

EXCEL POEM
= IF(you ask if it's worth corporate money, THEN I will lie to you, ELSE gain more weight)
= AND(look for ways to hide the hypertension in my neck and hands, discover the relaxation of television hypnosis)
= OR(bury myself in fantasies of living without headaches, stop strategizing in the shower, binge drink myself even fatter)
= LOOKUP(an estranged friend, between meetings and sitcoms, twice, but never call from lack of motivation)
= CONCATENATE(false handshakes, borrowed optimism, cases of beer)
<u>U</u>ndo it all, start over,   a blank cell.
=

Lady Liberty

She's reading the taboo literature

of the dead, stroking punk rock,

refusing to drone, inserting psychosis

into the office. Frank O'Hara's poems

vibrate between her legs.

Forget the condom! Release the breasts

of America!

Analysis

The psychiatrist taps his pencil to his chin.

I begin:

At first, I didn't understand
my coworkers' language,

or their devotion
to their jobs,

(or the commuters
who surrounded my car,

waiting for me to hesitate,
waiting to pounce

on any opportunity
to leave me behind)

the chattering, the hand gestures,
the small talk…

I'm fluent now.

He responds:

It sounds like a persistently
disturbing preoccupation
with occupation.

I nod and raise my eyebrow:

My laundry churns
in laundry
*   baskets*

because I'm afraid
to put it in drawers.

He motions for more.

I think I work
in order to feel
useful and needed.

He asks:

Does it define you?

and I shrug:

I don't go to bed at night
because I have to get up
in the morning.

He stares silently.

I give in to his silence:

It defines me
because I conform
to the desire for a pat on the back,
a condescending nod, a small dose
of thank you.

He persists:

What do you really want?

And I answer:

Something dropped
mistakenly down the drain

(swirling around the sink
like a roulette ball)

a diamond
waiting for me to find it
in the scummy, dead-skin
trap.

Transcription of a Doctor's Appointment

I slept through work today

to shake a fever and this television hemorrhoid.

I was prescribed anti-anxiety pills,

having kept my arms folded at the doctor's:

a defensive posture

against accusations, downsizing, ejaculation,

suicide, and knives.

Self Portrait
To Ginsberg

Don't read into this, Allen. I just want to talk.

I'm listening to Vietnam protest songs,
meditating through my anxiety and my need for approval
from executives and peers.

I'm conflicted.

No one drinks beer on Tuesday afternoons anymore.
But I keep hearing your voice
reading to yawning 1980's audiences, desensitized by television
and repetitive sex.

Apathy is spreading, Allen; I pick at mine
like a bleeding mole.

My home is too comfortable. My neighbors
don't look at me
on the way to their cars in the morning.
The convenience is overwhelming. No one stops long enough
to see themselves reflected
in office windows or flat-screen TV's.

I'm one of them.

I wait all year for three-day-weekends and W-2's. Weeks
roll over me like waves of nausea.
Now I'm going to Las Vegas. I've given up
trying to get away from it all.

Why are you so quiet?

My shoes are gaping at the soles. I won't replace them.

Everyone comments when I walk up the stairs
in my business casual attire. They ask
why I don't just buy a new pair.

Here, Allen, is my protest, my unbuyable expression of outrage.

Why aren't you with me?

WHERE DO THE SUICIDES GO?

Death of a Coworker

The opening hymn was call and response.

We stood, sat, and stood again.

I heard crying when his mother reluctantly announced

that he had taken his own life. It was then

that I realized the significance of his trembling hands

as we talked at my desk the week before.

Two pews away,

a little girl untied the white bow on her dress

and tied it up again.

Dedication
To Weldon Kees

For Ann, the lover.
For Ann, the tortured, the nervous,
the abandoned.

For Ann, the plain.
For Ann the tempted embracer,
silent by the water.

For Ann, the whisperer
of quiet jazz, extending her hand
and her insanity.

For Ann, the estranged mourner,
the holder of secret poems,
the owner of the intimate.

For Weldon, the tortured,
the waiting, the unquiet writer
of secrets. For Weldon,

the naked.

Where Do the Suicides Go?

Nurske said they become crows and bees,
and Dante rooted them
in the seventh circle
with nests of thieving harpies. But

maybe those who efface themselves
are actually resting, as if on a black
and modest shelf, forgiven,
with everyone else wondering

where they've gone, wondering
if death is the end, or if it's just the process
of making mistakes
until they find a way
                                of correcting themselves.

Scribbling

No one goes to the asylum for scribbling
in journals or masturbating
anymore.
After all, what harm can come
from scribbling?

Friday Night Binge

Along the wall of the Lamprey River Mill,
sand bags dry out. The half-octagonal shape
of the dam has controlled the river's black crest.

At home, I watch gangster movies.
Sunlight leaks into window-shaped squares
on the carpet, and the cat stalks sparrow-shadows.

Like an informant found floating in the Hudson,
I'm pale, bloated in the belly, and my mouth
gapes. Although some roads

have re-opened, I stay inside, clinging
to restraint's last dry rock. The smell of rain
is on the air again, and I'm all out of favors.

Lifecycle of a Wasp's Nest

The branch growing through me
rooted once
in June's sandy soil. Each gray strip

of my fabric exterior
was chewed into pulp, smoothed
and pasted by female workers in humid August.

Others guarded my exterior,
protecting the larvae
of my loves, my pre-sleep fantasies,

my erections. Each harvested offspring
later freeing itself
through the same valve by which it entered.

But in November, my warm weather purpose
served and ended, I wait
to be knocked to the ground
                        with a broomstick.

feeding cycle of the clock:

at 3:00am on sunday

i woke with the blissful un-obligated whim of a labrador
released by old age and the end of hunting season
                    no longer burdened by sunrise

at 3:00am on monday

i woke with the weight of predatory cats on my chest
in the crystalline blue light of the alarm clock's blinking colon
                  and various growling punctuation marks

at 3:00am on tuesday

i woke to the sound of enamel rubbing hungry enamel
like the un-oiled hinge of our back door swinging
                  in fall's predawn frost

at 3:00am on wednesday

i was torn open by scavengers
who nosed through the rotting leftovers of my repose
                  and left limping into the trees

at 3:00am on thursday

i cowered under the circling flight of bats
chirping, salivating and ingesting
                  the bloody morsels of my dreams

at 3:00am on friday

i searched blindly for nourishment
grubbing in the grassy darkness
                  and spreading the dirt with my boney fingers

but saturday

with the brush of her hand
domesticated and shadowed

> in the muted silver haze of moon

i slept

> without looking at the clock

During Sleep

During sleep, I make promises
I am not obliged
to keep. Desire reveals her pale and smooth thigh

as sunflowers watch
like the black outline of prophets
above the headboard.

Her eyes and fingers crawl across my skin
like the tones of a harpsichord,
and the moon reveals reflections of eastern women

leaping into lakes
at the prospect of wine.
My lover's face is no longer her own,

and my intentions are no longer innocent.
It's easy to pull the trigger when my weapon
is pointed at the back of her head,

and the painting keeps changing from roses
to blood spatter
to roses.

POEMS OF THE LOST

Crystal

She spoke in broken metaphors,
holding each word up with smoke

and spreading the cracks in her lips
the way Jesus stretched himself toward the sky

revealing the lash marks on his back.

House Arrest

I obsessed over the lives of teenagers
on Beverly Hills 90210. I envied

their resistance to cigarettes and rum drinks.
I kept spatulas and sauce pans

under my bed. I found a boyfriend.
Despite his speed addiction and the gun shots

in his neighborhood, I moved in.
I became a morning regular at the liquor store.

First, I drank to calm my nerves before a test,
then for no reason. I blacked out

weekly. One morning, I woke up blonde
and laughed. He kicked me out.

I hid my addiction and moved back home.
I kept bottles under my bed.

I thought no one would notice the missing
red wine or empty Budweiser cans.

I blacked out daily. I lit my car on fire.
I hated the screeching noise it made.

I lit a friend's apartment building on fire
because I couldn't afford to pay the rent.

To avoid jail time, I took advantage of family-
connections and pity.

I embraced probation. Why wouldn't I
violate it? I already felt like a prisoner.

Amnesia

I'm blonde today. No one noticed.
So I lingered
outside an office,

waited for sweet-smelling women
to walk by in suits, pretended
I was one of them. Security

guards escorted me
to the subway and left bruises
on my arm. I enjoyed the attention.

I don't know who I am.
I wait in line with filthy men
for my dinner.

I avoid eye contact, always
staring at my plate. I can't talk
to my family. I thought

I recognized my brother
on the street yesterday, but I couldn't
speak. He kept walking.

I didn't catch his eye.
I looked regretfully
into yellow living room windows

last night. I remembered
calling him "Bud", watching
America's Funniest Videos

and laughing. Everyone's
a stranger now. Everyone
judges me. That's why I obsess

over eye liner, bite my nails,
smoke Marlboro Lights, and drink
whisky until I vomit. That's why

DREAMING AGAIN

I sleep in parking garages
and unlocked cars. That's why
I dream of being home again.

Buttered Popcorn

I Google my sister's name about once a month now,

usually when I sit down with a bowl of popcorn

to watch TV. I remember when the carpet was shag blue

and we watched syndicated episodes of the Brady Bunch together.

As Bobby and Cindy accused each other of stealing,

she lay back on the twin bed, her head propped up by pillows.

We ate buttered popcorn from an aluminum mixing bowl.

When Cindy's new trophy drove Bobby to jealously

enter an ice-cream-eating contest, we laughed.

We avoided the grayness of March. Bobby and Cindy,

brother and sister, but not by blood, were lost

in the Grand Canyon. I was twenty, but remembered laughing

with her twelve years earlier. I haven't seen her since that day.

I went out with friends, and she left while no one was home.

I found her note folded neatly into a square on the coffee table.

I wondered if it was a suicide note, and I looked for her body

in the basement, bathrooms, bedrooms. I didn't find her.

Ten years later, at thirty, I watched as Bobby and Cindy were rescued

before nightfall. Everything worked out for the Bradys in the end.

I turned off the television and carried the bowl to the sink.

The unpopped kernels scratched and swished in salt.

Snipes

20 Marlboros / smoked in restaurant bathrooms / and private alleyways /
quarters quietly taken from mom's purse / slid secretly / into the machine /

the pack found by my father / resulting in his lecture / and my sister's lies /
thrown into the trash / without a back-up plan / an unsatisfied craving /

3 Marlboros / stolen from Uncle Paul's pack / one at a time /
her sideways exhale / through a cracked window / she was willing /

to risk discovery / determined to defy / maturing her contempt /
she anticipated shouting matches / punishments / the tension of silence /

1 Marlboro / already half smoked / picked carefully from an ash tray /
a bent cigarette / stale and used / to satisfy her teenage addiction /

she was ashtray hunting / anything for a drag / searching the ground /
for a snipe / twisted into pavement / the taste of a stranger's spit /

My Aluminum Baseball Bat

I never actually hit anyone with it,
but I was great at puffing out my chest
and cocking the bat, or leaning on it
as if to say, "I know you see my bat,
and I know you know I'll use it."
I was thirteen, and I didn't think
that anyone noticed my trembling hands.

The first time I might have brandished it,
our neighbor, Tom, was yelling at my mother.
She had made a comment about his drinking
and yelling at night with the windows open.
Tom pointed a finger at my mother's face,
but she stood firmly in the doorway, and I stood
firmly behind her, one hand clutching my bat.

The true test came later that summer.
My sister's boyfriend
shouted at her through the screen door
as his friends waited in the car.
Once again, I rushed to my room for the bat,
tucked in a bag under my glove.
I sweated with the anticipation

of busting into the street, maybe breaking
the windshield to send them peeling away.
When I came downstairs, he was crouching
beside her car, jabbing its tires with a knife.
I stopped stiff in the doorway, watching him
finish and drive away laughing. Later,
my sister hugged me as I cried.

My Sister's Face

Turning away from a homeless woman
sleeping on Boston Common was turning away
from my sister's violent hangover as I watched
her son play in the back yard.

Or pouring washer fluid into the well of my car
with the same precision she used to pour water
into our father's whisky bottle, bringing
it level with the line he'd drawn on the label

after her first relapse. Dunking my head
in the ocean resembled the time she jumped
into our pool to hide her intoxication after driving
with her three-year-old in the back seat.

I pretend to disown her in these memories,
just like she pretended to throw me a baseball,
faking over and over until she finally hit my nose,
sending me bloodied and crying into the house.

Letter of Resignation

Dear friend, when you believed I was changing,
I am sorry to say, I was lying.

I'm not sure whether I invented these
details to please you or to please myself.

Months ago, I decided I would leave.
I formed a plan that you could never see.

I resolved that this time I would hurt you
as little as possible. It's true.

I imagined that you wanted pity.
I imagined you grateful for mercy.

Despite your true feelings, as I depart
I request only that you lie to me.

Lie to me with the same sincerity
I have extended again and again.

ABOUT THE AUTHOR

Martin Elwell is a New Hampshire-based poet and editor. He co-edited *Bearers of Distance*, an anthology of poems by runners from Eastern Point Press, and he is News & Resources Editor for *The Found Poetry Review*. You can find him on Twitter @MartyElwell, read his poems at http://martinelwell.wordpress.com and follow his travels at http://wordspergallon.com.

54034792R00024

Made in the USA
Lexington, KY
30 July 2016